101 VIDEO MARKETING TIPS AND STRATEGIES

For Small Businesses

Lasse Rouhiainen

www.LasseRouhiainen.com

Please Review This Book

Please take a moment to review my book on Amazon. All of your feedback will help make any revisions (or potentially a sequel) even better than the original

Content

TABLE OF CONTENTS:
101 VIDEO MARKETING TIPS AND STRATEGIES
FOR SMALL BUSINESSES

Introduction

Are you leveraging the full potential of online video marketing on 2014?

Do you know how to implement powerful video marketing strategies and promote your business using video marketing?

Most small and medium sizes companies are unaware of the huge power of using video as a tool to improve credibility and confidence towards your customers and to teach and educate them about the benefits of your products.

There are a lot of information on video marketing online, however most small business owners, marketers and business professionals find video marketing somewhat confusing as there are too many option as to how to start, which camera to choose, what to say on a video and how to promote your video on YouTube?

I wrote this book to help you to have a clear list of the most important topics related to video marketing and I divided them into 101 very easy to understand quick tips and avoided the use of theoretical scenarios and wanted to provide clear strategies you can take action immediately after reading the book.

The book is divided into five sections:

SECTION 1: PLANNING

SECTION 2: RECORDING

SECTION 3: YOUTUBE PROMOTION

SECTION 4: ADDITIONAL VIDEO STRATEGIES

SECTION 5: IPHONE VIDEO MARKETING STRATEGIES

And each of these are divided into 5 sub sections and each sub section has 4 tips and strategies.

You might enjoy taking time to review the table of content and maybe start from the part, which is most crucial or needed for your business, or read from start to finish.

The purpose of this book is to save you countless hours you could be spending on planning and trying to figure out how to start producing videos that are impactful and improve your online presence.

In 2014 and beyond, consumers are all the time more and more distracted and they have a very short attention span. Therefore, my recommendation is to create short videos and to be concise in your communication. Additionally, its becoming more important to edit your videos in a professional way and try to make them entertaining.

I hope you enjoy learning about different video marketing tips and wish you a great success applying them.

Good luck,

Lasse Rouhiainen

www.lasserouhiainen.com

email: lasse@lasserouhiainen.com

I recommend to signup on my newsletter at *www.lasserouhiainen.com* in order to receive the tips and strategies on video marketing and social media.

Let's get started since the clients are waiting for you...

Small Businesses Are Struggling and They Need Your Help

SECTION 1: PLANNING

Planning – Preparation

1. What is the main objective of your videos?

The first step in the video marketing plan is identifying your main objectives for creating the videos and deciding how results will be measured. For example, most new tech startup companies will set a primary objective of impressing possible investors or venture capitalists to solicit funding.

For a typical small business, one of the main objectives should include increasing the company's credibility and confidence among consumers. This market recognition will help a business to sell more while also building trust with potential clients. Take the time to carefully decide what the company's main objective will be when it comes to video marketing.

2. Who are your ideal clients?

Don't try to make your videos appeal to everyone. Instead, focus them directly towards your potential customers. In order to achieve this, carefully answer the following questions:

- What are the age, gender, and hobbies of your ideal client?

- What is the main problem your ideal client wants to solve?

- What emotional needs the idea customer has related to the problem?

- What keywords does your ideal customer search for on sites such as Google and other search engine?

These are just some of the questions that will help you focus and get clarity on why you are making your videos. For instance, an urban gym for females can create videos targeting young single females who want to attract a partner and improve their bodies. In this example, the main problem for them to focus on would be "improving one's body" and the emotional need would be "finding an ideal partner".

3. Who records your videos and when?

This part is simple but many times overlooked by companies. In order to achieve positive results, I normally advise companies to create at least 10 or 20 videos. Decide who will be responsible for planning, shooting, editing, promoting and analyzing the results of your company's videos. Some bigger companies will have a community manager who is responsible for this, while smaller companies typically outsource this work to a social media consultant or manager. Additionally, you should clarify when the videos will be recorded. As companies are constantly needing to produce new and interesting content, I suggest being consistent - try to upload new videos every week or every other week. This might at first sound daunting, but remember that your efforts will generate great results when done correctly. Time can be saved by quickly creating videos using Smartphones, such as the iPhone or Droid.

4. What is your budget?

To achieve great results, you need to invest money into your video marketing. There are several strategies to help save on costs; however, it's recommended that you invest in a quality camera and some accessories to separate your company from the competition.

Your budget will also depend on the type of company and, in particular, the ideal targeted clients. For example, for law firms or accountants who would like to create videos sharing interesting tips related to their work, I would recommend buying a Canon Rebel Ti3 digital SLR camera (or similar) to create high-quality full-HD videos. In contrast, a small 2-star hotel could utilize the Sony Bloggie. More on choosing the right video camera for your needs will be discussed later in this book.

Market research – the most powerful online tools

5. Google Keyword Tool and Google Trends

Earlier in this book, I mentioned 'defining your ideal customer'. The next step is to identify the main keywords these customers type on Google so that you can create videos optimizing on these searches. The most well-known free tool to do this is Google Keyword Reach Tool, which can be found at:

https://adwords.google.com/select/KeywordToolExternal

Simply go to this site and type in both your sector and geographical area. For instance, if you are a restaurant owner in Denver, Colorado, USA, you would type "restaurant Denver" in the search box.

The following is a sample list generated by this search, and how you can go about selecting the relevant search parameters for your company:

☑	restaurants in denver ▾	Low	135,000	135,000
☐	best restaurants in denver ▾	Low	18,100	18,100
☐	fruition **restaurant denver** ▾	Low	260	210
☐	oldest restaurant in denver ▾	Low	210	210
☐	bones **restaurant denver** ▾	Low	260	260
☐	jerusalem **restaurant denver** ▾	Low	320	260
☐	prima **restaurant denver** ▾	Low	260	210
☐	tamayo **restaurant denver** ▾	Low	170	170
☑	romantic restaurants in denver ▾	Medium	1,300	1,300
☐	altitude **restaurant denver** ▾	Low	480	480
☐	fuel **restaurant denver** ▾	Low	170	170
☑	nice restaurants in denver ▾	Medium	720	720

6. How to expand your keyword list with Übersuggest

In addition to Google Keyword Tool, you may wish to use Übersuggest. This is yet another great free tool which helps expand keyword lists. By using this program you can get more ideas of what topics your customers are searching for online.

Basically, Ubersuggest takes your generic search terms (like "restaurant Denver"), adds a letter or a digit in front of it, and then generates suggestions. For the example we've been using, "restaurant Denver", this tool generates 364 variations. Your job is then to pick the ones best related to your company or products. Again, choose the most relevant keywords and later film one video for each.

URL: *http://ubersuggest.org*

7. Discover questions your customers type on Google

Some of the most powerful videos are those where you directly answer your ideal customer's questions and doubts. Wordtracker provides a tool to list the most commonly typed questions.

You can find this program at:

https://freekeywords.wordtracker.com/keyword-questions

For instance, a chiropractor could simply search the word "chiropractic". When conducting this search myself, I received the following results:

Results for: *Chiropractic*	Download

	Question	Times asked (?)
1	chiropractic powered by wordpress leave a comment name required	75
2	how many people think chiropractic works?	20
3	chiropractic enter yourname@yourkeywords in the name field keywordluv website -comments are	15
4	chiropractic [img] code is on	14
5	what is chiropractic	13
6	chiropractic care do they need to x-ray	12
7	chiropractic commentluv leave a reply website -comments are closed	11
8	how chiropractic wellness is beneficial to your health	10
9	how chiropractic services be beneficial to you	10
10	what chiropractic is and how it can help you	10
11	what chiropractic wellness is and how it can help you	10
12	studies have shown that chiropractic care can help decrease many of the symptoms of pms	10
13	chiropractic wilness and how it can help you	10

From this list I would pick up interesting questions such as "how chiropractic wellness is beneficial to your health" and "what chiropractic is and how it can help you". These would be great topics for video titles on YouTube because you always need to educate and share valuable information related to your target market.

Today in order to use this tool you need to signup for a trial account on WordTracker:

https://original.wordtracker.com

Results for: *Chiropractic*

Question
1   chiropractic powered by wordpress leave a comment name required
2   how many people think chiropractic works?
3   chiropractic enter yourname@yourkeywords in the name field keywordluv website -comments are
4   chiropractic [img] code is on
5   what is chiropractic
6   chiropractic care do they need to x-ray
7   chiropractic commentluv leave a reply website -comments are closed
8   how chiropractic wellness is beneficial to your health
9   how chiropractic services be beneficial to you
10   what chiropractic is and how it can help you
11   what chiropractic wellness is and how it can help you
12   studies have shown that chiropractic care can help decrease many of the symptoms of pms
13   chiropractic wliness and how it can help you

8. Find interesting topics and questions on Quora

When creating a social media or video marketing plan, I often visit Quora.com. This is a fantastic social network built around the idea that anyone can ask questions on any topic. All of the questions and answers are organized into specific categories. Quora is widely used among tech professionals, however, you can find a lot of great questions and answers for any type of company.

For instance, if you search "car repair" you can find a big list of interesting questions listed within this category:

http://www.quora.com/Auto-Repair

"How do I know if my battery or alternator is bad?" and "Can I leave a car for a year without driving and just jump it a year later?"

These would be awesome videos for a car repair company who wants to convey valuable and useful information in their videos. This site may be found by visiting: URL:

http://www.quora.com

Video planning – What kind of videos should your company create?

9. Company presentation

In this day and age, every company should have a video presentation on their main website that properly conveys what the company wishes to achieve and the products or services it will provide for a specific target market. The easiest way to quickly produce this kind of video is by using a service like Animoto.com that creates a slideshow video. However, the most professional video presentations are those in which company employees talk or present themselves; this format generates more credibility than a simple slideshow video. Such presentations can include a discussion of who the company is, how their products and/or services can be found, and the benefits they bring to the market. You can also use a new tool called VideoLean. As a reader of this book you have a -15% discount of using VideoLean when using this link:

http://social.videolean.com/

10. Employee presentation videos

Most online consumers distrust companies and the promises made in their sales messages. Consequently, you need to show the public that behind your brand there are authentic people who truly care about their customers and are willing to serve their needs. Most service companies should encourage their employees who deal with customer contact and relations to appear in these videos.

The familiarity created by smiling faces and real employee presentation will help a customer to feel personally linked the company, its services and products. This in turn will generate more credibility to the company as well as help the customers to become more brand loyal. In these videos, employees can share such things as their name and position within the company, their relation to customer services, and how they can be reached.

11. Questions and answers videos

Probably the easiest and fastest way to produce interesting videos from a potential customer's point of view is by creating a series of "Q&A" videos, answering the most frequently asked questions. For example a wellness center could gather all of the most popular customer questions asked before making purchases, and then creating a series of videos answering one question per video.

For most business owners, this might seem too easy. However, from a potential customer's point of view, providing this vital information lets them know your company cares about their problems. In turn, the company is also benefited by lowering the amount of customer service inquiries received. By creating 10 videos based on frequently asked questions, a company will also generate material that many potential buyers are searching online, since many people type questions into search engines like YouTube and Google.

12. Testimonial videos

Perhaps the most powerful, and yet often times overlooked, aspect of an influential video presentation needs to revolve around customer testimonials. As there exist thousands of companies all purporting to be marketing the best product, what real life customers have to say is fast becoming the pivotal factor in determining a company's success.

Nevertheless, you should be aware that online consumers might also be suspicious of video testimonials appearing too generic or full of adjectives and hype. Testimonials should always be authentic, real, and clearly communicate customers' experiences with the product. One way to achieve this is by using "before and after" testimonials, or videos where customers show their real results obtained. For example, a consulting agency may ask its clients to prepare a video showing some real results or an empirical improvement in their numbers. One effective way of gathering video testimonials is by encouraging customers to send in their own video testimonials or presentations of using the products.

Video planning – What kind of videos your company should create? Part II

13. Educational and Tutorial

Educational and tutorial style videos are two of the most powerful types a company can make. Most people go to sites like YouTube and Google to learn something or to find a solution to their problem, so by creating these videos you also create a presence in those search results. The more you educate your target audience, the closer they will move towards you and your product. Customers will also begin to perceive you as an expert in the field and line of product or services, again generating more consumer confidence. Educational and tutorial videos should be short and simple, with an emphasis on the most important information. They should also give clear action items to the viewer. An example could be a real estate agent listing the necessary paperwork to sell a home, or a hotel owner presenting the most interesting places to visit near his hotel. The more educational content you produce, the more you can separate yourself from the competition and be viewed as an expert within your field.

14. Screen capture

"Screen capture videos" are when you record the screen images of one's computer together with the audio of the person speaking. These kinds of videos are very common among software companies who need video tutorials on how to use their programs.

Screen capture videos are a great way to produce interesting content quickly, particularly for business owners who feel uncomfortable in front of a camera. This is especially so for service companies such as consulting agencies, law firms, and accountants. This style of video is far more effective than one where the presenter might seem awkward on screen. Some business owners are able to explain key points much more confidently by not worrying about their appearance. At some point you should try to show your face in the videos, but screen capture videos are a great way to grow more comfortable with the process. Screen capture often works better as a means of instruction, more so than a text manual, as the steps will often be more easy to follow in a visual form. The two most widely used programs for screen capture videos are Camtasia for PCs and Screenflow for Macs.

15. Video Interviews

Often times the hardest part in beginning this process is coming up with new ideas for your company videos. Video interviews can be a great answer for producing content quickly, without having to develop creative content. A restaurant owner can interview his chef or some of the restaurant's most frequent visitors. A hotel manager can interview a local tourism official to share tips on which places to visit.

Video interviews don't often need as much preparation as other types of videos, but they do require three key elements to make an impact - an introduction, interesting questions, and a strong conclusion. Video interviews connect to consumers on a very human level as talking in an interview appears far more natural than when presenting an educational video. Within this more natural presentation style, it's often easier to get across important information.

Video interviews should then primarily focus on sharing valuable content and tips with the target audience.

16. Storytelling videos

Storytelling is a natural way for human beings to convey complex information and make sense of things. Therefore, storytelling videos can be the most inspiring type of videos for all small companies to present their products and services. This holds particularly true for videos presented by a business's founder who either built it from the ground up with little money and resources, or whose business has become successful after many setbacks. Storytelling videos are particularly impactful when the presenter incorporates humor, or can relate witty stories revolving around his or her business. Most importantly, a storytelling video can present a company's values and how incorporating those values helped the business to become successful. The following are a few ideas to help spark your creativity and develop interesting stories you can share in your videos: What is the funniest thing that has happened to you in your business? What was the most difficult challenge in your career and what did you learn from it? Why are you doing what you are doing? This last suggestion is a bit more complex and, to properly explore its potential, I highly recommend reviewing my friend Ridgely Goldsborough book, "Why Marketing Formula," in which he teaches business owners to discover their "why".

Video planning – What kind of videos you should make – Part III

17. Create videos by using the formula "your business + geographical location"

As you can see from keyword research tools such as Google's "Keyword Tool", many consumers search keywords which include the (1) type of business and (2) geographical location. For example, "Restaurant Denver", as used in the previous example where I showed how to use Google Keyword Tool.

It's somewhat difficult to rank at the top of a Google search with this kind of generic keyword - you will be going up against a lot of competition from huge Internet portals like tripadvisor.com and yelp.com. However, many of your potential clients also search on YouTube and, over there, you can rank your video at the top by applying the YouTube optimization strategies discussed later on in this book.

For optimizing your videos on YouTube, you should create approximately 3 videos targeting keywords like "your business + geographical location". This form of optimization yields valuable results and can generate a lot of business.

18. Create videos about your events or those you participate in

If your company is organizing any events, these should be recorded on video and uploaded. Videos like these make for great content on your website and YouTube channel.

You also have the option to create "live streaming" - transmitting a live video feed online from your event. Two of the most well-known companies providing this service are *http://new.livestream.com/* and *http://www.ustream.tv*. However, Google's own "Google Hangout" is getting better features all of the time and allows you to do free live streaming for an unlimited number of viewers. You can learn more about Google Hangouts here:

http://www.google.com/+/learnmore/hangouts/onair.html

19. Get your clients to record videos by organizing a video contest

One of the most powerful strategies for social media marketing is enticing your clients and audience to share your marketing messages with their own friends and peers on Social Networks. One way to achieve this is by uploading videos created by your clients showcasing or reviewing your products and services.

When planning a video contest, you should consider the following points:

- What will be the competition's rules (be as clear as possible)?

  - What will be the timeframe for participants submitting their content?

  - What will be the final prize and how will a winner be selected

  - What kind of videos should the participants create?

  - Etc...

The clearer you are with the rules, the better the results you will have. You can ask the participants to send their videos directly to your company or to upload them onto YouTube. The first option can be safer for your company because this way you can filter the videos and their content. Allowing participants to upload videos themselves poses the risk of harming your brand image some way.

Also, make sure to ask for written permission from the participants to use their videos in your marketing efforts.

A video contest is a great way to generate a lot of interesting and original video content. Nevertheless, you need to plan it correctly in order for it to be successful.

20. Create your video marketing plan

Over the years I have created many strategic video marketing plans for small and medium sized companies. I consider this to be the most essential part of your planning process.

Before you begin, please review all of the video marketing ideas I have presented thus far. Write down on a piece of paper all of the ideas you have brainstormed on doing these videos for your company.

Your video marketing plan should include at least one video in each of the categories mentioned earlier.

Here is an example of one video plan I had created for an e-commerce store client:

- 4 client testimonial videos

- 3 presentation videos of the employees

- 5 "how-to" tutorial videos

- 8 "Q&A" videos of frequently asked questions

- 4 slideshow videos (these can be quickly made using services like animation.com as covered later in this book - normally ranked with the formula "business + geographical location")

In total, that makes 24 videos. The company has 10 weeks to implement and create them all.

As you can see, the primary focus is on the "how to" tutorials and "FAQ" videos as these are normally the most useful content for potential clients.

Now it's time to create the video marketing plan for your company. Try to be as specific as possible and clearly write down all of your ideas. When just starting out, most of the videos can be only 1 to 1.5 minutes long - creating 5 or so videos in one day like this is much easier than you might think.

SECTION 2: RECORDING

Powerful advice for making your video stand out

In this section you will learn a few techniques on how to make your videos stand out and to be more effective. These are just some quick strategies you can apply; to learn more advanced video creation strategies, like creating the right story board, I recommend getting a copy of the book, "Shoot to Sell: Make Money Producing Special Interest Videos", by Rick Smith and Kim Miller.

21. Have a clear introduction as to what your videos are all about

There are a lot of great YouTube videos with only a few views due to the fact that the introduction is missing. This results in the viewer not being clear on the benefit of watching the video and therefore overlooking it entirely.

Remember, most of your audience is very busy and their lives are full of distractions. They might be watching your video with their smartphone or tablet on the bus or metro. Therefore, you need to clearly communicate what your video is all about and, in some cases, even add curiosity by teasing what you will reveal at the end of the video.

Some companies also create branded intros, which they place at the beginning of each video. If you opt to do this, make sure your intro is very short - not longer than 4 seconds. It might also be best to outsource the creation of this intro.

22. Create convincing "calls to action" on your videos

A "call to action" is one of the main elements that small and medium sized companies mistakenly don't include the right way. The term refers to encouraging the viewer to take same action after watching the video, like visit your website or share the video with their friends.

Depending on the topic of your video, you can use different calls to action in your videos, including:

– Visit your website

– Call your office number

– Signup for your company's newsletter

– Visit your business's Facebook page (and do something there like participate in a contest)

– Participate in your upcoming event or online conference

– Subscribe to your YouTube channel, share the video, and leave comments under the video.

– Etc..

As you can see, there are many different types of calls to action. Before making your video, you should be clear on the purpose of your video and what call to action you want to use.

Calls to action can be said on the video and also showed with text (which you can add when editing the video or using YouTube annotations). The bigger your promise on the call to action, the more people you will entice. For example, a law firm could create short "how to" tutorial videos and, at the end of each video, encourage the viewer to download a free white paper on their website to learn more.

This type of marketing, providing powerful free tips and strategies via video and written text to your audience, is a very powerful tool. Try to think how you can apply this to your business.

23. Common mistakes to avoid and making your videos

It's always useful to have a list of the common mistakes companies and businesses owners make with video marketing. Become familiar with these and avoid making them yourself:

– Use a background relevant to your business: Don't shoot videos next to a wall or in front of a background that has nothing to do with your business. Take the time to organize your surroundings in a manner that suits your business or the topic of your videos.

– Don't try to always be perfect in front of the camera: Today, consumers want to see authenticity; let your employees behave normally with all of their unique character and imperfections. Don't worry too much about trying to be perfect in front of the camera - just be yourself and dressed in the fashion that suits your business.

– Take care in positioning your frames: Try to frame the person speaking in the middle of your video and not too far away. It's difficult to make a connection with someone who is really far away in the shot. Try positioning close enough to see the color of their eyes.

– Don't act too nervous: If you get nervous, just think of the audience as one of your clients you just haven't met yet. Try taking deep breaths and relaxing your body before going in front of the camera.

– Use poor audio quality and bad lighting in your videos: At the end this might effect the online reputation of your company if you keep uploading a lot of videos with bad audio and bad lighting. To avoid this simply follow the strategies presented in this book where we talk about how to create professional audio and lighting for your videos.

24. Learn to use NLP in your videos

NLP, or "neuro-linguistic programming", can drastically improve the effectiveness and impact of your communication with clients.

One example of applying NLP in your company's videos is by "talking about what will happen in the future". Credit to Harlan Kilstein for this technique. For instance, some hotels for which I have created video campaigns have successfully implemented this strategy by having an employee say something to the effect of:

"Hi, my name is _____ and I work here at _____ hotel. When you come here you can find me at my table in the lobby and I can help you to _____"

Basically, the idea is for the employee to talk about "what will happen in the future" so the viewer will start to create a mental image and visualize him or herself visiting the hotel.

NLP is very powerful when applied to marketing but is too big of a topic to cover in this book. I recommend picking up a basic book on this topic and studying it further. Always consider how to apply it in your videos.

Options for choosing the right video camera

When it comes to selecting the right camera for recording your business's videos, I recommend always trying to record in HD (high definition). This improved level of quality will better showcase your business in a more professional manner and also help to separate yourself from the competition. The following is a list of different cameras you might consider with HD capabilities. If you like making these videos and plan on devoting more resources to their production, you might even considering purchasing several of them for various purposes.

25. Canon Rebel tI3

To produce professional quality videos within a minimal budget (under $600 USD), the best choice would be the Canon Rebel Ti3. It records very high quality videos; even some TV series have been recorded with this camera. This model is perfect for any company wishing to document conferences and meetings, such as law firms, accounting offices, or consultants. It's also very highly recommended for any company with high-end clients, for example 4 or 5 star hotels or upscale wellness centers. The Canon Rebel Ti3 is the camera I personally use to record most of my videos and to obtain professional production. I might also recommend using the EF 50mm f/1.8 II lense by Canon (thanks to Gideon Shalwick for this find and many other video marketing strategies I have learned from him) to reduce blurring and improve focus. The only downside to this camera is that it takes some time to learn how to use the right settings and, therefore, is not as simple to use as some other options - like the iPhone.

26. GoPro

GoPro is a very professional quality camera that can easily fit in the palm of your hand. It was made primarily for sport videographers who wanted to record fast-paced videos. This camera can film up to 60 frames per second and is very useful for any small business in the health and wellness sector, such as gyms, excursion companies, spas, and dance studios. The latest version of GoPro Hero3 comes with wifi capability built in, allowing for simple and fast uploading of your videos onto sites like YouTube and instant sharing of still frames online. It can even link with your Smartphone through Android or iPhone apps to be used remotely.

27. iPhone

By far one of the cameras I am most excited about lately is standard on the current iPhone models. This is especially so because of the many video applications now available on the app market. This tends to be my most commonly recommended camera when consulting new businesses, as it provides for the ability to record in full-HD, is always carried on your person, and the videos are extremely easy to edit through various applications. You can also then upload directly onto sites such as YouTube without intermediary steps necessary with other cameras.

More and more business owners these days are turning to Smartphones for their video recording needs because of these features. Later in this book we will cover in more depth the necessary video marketing applications for the iPhone as well as video equipment you should purchase. All types of small businesses should consider learning to record high quality videos with the iPhone, particularly because of its comparable speed to other camera options.

28. Sony Bloggie

Sony Bloggie is a good quality pocket camcorder, able to film in 1080p HD with web-friendly capabilities, that can be found for under $140 USD on various discounted sellers (such as Amazon.com). With its USB connection, the videos can be quickly uploaded online. And, due to its small size, this camera is also very portable and can be taken with you almost anywhere. However, for most business owners, I still advise using the Canon Rebel or iPhone for producing higher quality videos and ease in editing your final product.

Video Creation tools and programs

29. Record professional screen captures with Screenflow (Mac)

As a Mac user, my favorite screen recording program is Screenflow. This particular program is very fast, easy to use, and provides a variety of great options when editing your screen recordings. Screenflow can record your computer screen images and any actions you perform on it, and even your face via webcam to make your tutorials more human. Additionally, you can add callouts, texts, annotations, and improve the audio or video quality of your recordings.

The latest version of Screenflow - Screenflow 4 - allows you to quickly do both basic and advanced editing, and even has a chroma key support. One of the main benefits for editing your videos with Screenflow is that it's much faster than other editing software, like iMovie or FinalCut. Screenflow comes with a $99 USD price tag, but you can get the free trial version for 30 days to test it out.

All small businesses with intangible products, such as service businesses, should create educational screen recording tutorials. Screenflow is also great for demonstrating the capabilities of a particular software product, or explaining certain key concepts and ideas to customers.

30. Camtasia and Jing (PC)

Camtasia is maybe the most well-known screen recording program. Camtasia has many of the same features as Screenflow, and can be utilized on either a PC or Mac. As with Screenflow, a trial version is available to test its functions, while the full version is available for $299 USD (for the PC).

TechSmith, creator of Camtasia, has also put out a great product called Jing Project. This is deal for business owners and companies just getting started with video recording. This free software allows you to quickly record video tutorials under 5 minutes long (Camtasia can take videos of any length), best suited for companies looking for practice with this process who don't want to immediately invest in Screenflow or Camtasia. This software works on both Macs and PCs, which I personally use often for recording quick clips to send to clients or for collaborations via email.

31. Create great looking slideshows with Animoto or VideoLean

Probably the quickest way to create videos for small businesses is through slideshow videos. Take photos and video clips, accompany them with some music, and turn the final show into a marketing masterpiece. Animoto.com is the most well-know program for this, with several professional templates and copyright free music that you can quickly access and incorporate to produce great looking slideshow videos.

Unfortunately, Animoto is quickly being discovered and popularized among marketers, making slideshows produced through them less unique or set apart from the competition. Therefore, I would suggest Video Lean - my favorite tool. Like Animoto, this is another online tool with templates and music, but is still yet undiscovered by many marketers or companies. Use the link social.videolean.com for 15% discount.

Every small business should have at least one slideshow video presenting their business. However, I don't recommend presenting all your videos in this fashion, as consumers want to both see and hear the people behind the business.

32. Surprise your ideal clients with great looking animated videos - Goanimate.com and Aniboom.com

Especially among tech start-up companies, animated videos are commonly used to present products and services. Typical animated videos are approximately 1 to 1.5 minutes in length and present both the "problem" and "solution". By signing up for free on Goanimate.com, you can gain access to the most basic trial version allowing you to quickly create animated videos along with tutorials, learning how to get started with characters, backgrounds, and even music. GoAnimate also offers a wide variety of animation tools and settings for paid subscription clients should you want to produce a series of animated videos.

To produce more professional looking animation for your company videos, you may want to check out Aniboom.com. This site provides a portal to freelance graphic artists providing offers to create unique, personalized animation for your company. All you have to do is post a detailed description of the kind of video you want - desired length, storyline, and an approximate budget. Aniboom's team reviews your criteria and posts the job on their wall for you. All you have to do then is pick the animator you want and watch your animation come to life before your very eyes. It might be a good idea to start with a short 30 – 60 second video and to review animated videos by other companies to get some ideas for your own business. URL:

www.animoto.com and www.aniboom.com

Video equipment options

33. Make your video frames more stable by using a tripod

It's important that videos where you have someone talking to a camera don't look shaky. This would include video interviews, employee presentations, storytelling videos, etc. Most of the cameras recommended earlier can be easily connected to a tripod. Perhaps the most well-known brand is Manfrotto. If you are recording someone sitting at an office table, you might want to consider using a mini tripod with telescoping legs which, when expanded, is normally 8" tall.

When using a tripod, make sure that your video camera lens is positioned at eye height of the person speaking. This particular angle will improve the quality and presentation of your video.

34. Improve video quality by using an external microphone

Some experts contend that audio quality accounts for 60% - 70% of your video's overall success. Particularly nowadays when so many companies promote video content, it's fundamental that your videos always have high quality audio, avoiding disturbing background noises and other common audio problems.

Most cameras, like the Canon Rebel and GoPro Hero 3, have an input port for an external microphone. My favorite wireless external microphone by far is the Sony ECM-AW3, normally found for under $170 USD on discounted sites such as Amazon.com. This microphone works well with almost any camera, is lightweight, and ensures a nice quality audio. It even works with the iPhone if you use a connector - more about that later on in the iPhone section of this book.

If you are looking for a simple cable microphone, I would go for the Olympus ME-51S Stereo Microphone. Some video marketers use Rode Shotgun Mics, normally selling for under $200 USD.

35. Improve your videos' impact with extra lighting

For years, I was filming videos next to a window or some other area with good lighting. However, once I purchased a professional lighting kit, the quality of my recordings skyrocketed. On Amazon.com, you can find several studio lighting kits for under $200 USD that will help make your videos stand out from the crowd. You can even use the lighting to take professional photographs of your employees. This is a no-brainer for companies wanting to produce a large number of high-quality videos. You can even take the lighting with you on-location if needed.

36. Shoot professional Chroma key & Green-screen videos

Chroma key is a technique, which allows you to remove the background of your videos and replace it with a photo.

TV newscasting commonly utilizes chroma key for this purpose, and you can too in your own marketing videos.

You can begin by searching for "Chroma key green screen kit" on sites like Amazon.com, evaluating the various options for purchase. Many versions are available for under $200 USD along with the appropriate professional lighting kits. This equipment will allow you to record your videos with a green screen background that, in a postproduction phase, will be replaced with another image of your choosing.

Most professional video editing programs - such as iMovie, Final Cut Pro for Mac, Sony Vegas, and Adobe Premiere - allow you to perform chroma key effects while editing. The latest version of Screenflow (version 4) also has this feature. As this program is typically faster than other editing programs for the Mac, I use this one myself for all editing.

37. Learn to use the video editing program most suited to your needs

To ensure that your videos always look professional, you can use video editing tools to add your company logo, titles, intros, or other effects. As mentioned in the introduction of this book I think professional video editing will be a crucial activity that will set companies apart from the crowd.

INTERVIEW WITH GIDEON SHALWICK

In this next section my friend and video marketing expert, Gideon Shalwick shares why he thinks video editing and creating animated introductions for your videos are so important

Why do you recommend marketers to focus on editing their videos more on 2014?

A cleverly edited video can make a massive difference in the level of engagement you get from your videos.

Imagine two scenarios…

In scenario 1, you're watching a talking head kind of video, of a presenter teaching you how to change the oil in your car. In this case, there is no editing and all you can see and hear is the presenter's face and voice.

Now imagine scenario 2, where it's exactly the same presenter, but this time, the video is complimented with some nice b-rolls visually showing you how to change the oil of the car, the content is broken up into logical sections with professional segueways helping you transition between the sections, and also some nice music to help set the right emotion for the video.

Which video do you think will be more engaging to watch and as a result will have a much better chance of getting a lot more views? The second one of course!

This is just a simple example, but it illustrates how a simple video can be made a lot more engaging with just some very simple additions in the video editing.

As a video content marketer, getting people engaged, and keeping their attention is THE MOST IMPORTANT thing you can do for your videos. And spending a little bit more time on the planning and editing of your videos can make a massive difference.

Why do you think its important to use intros and Segueways today when doing video marketing?

In today's competitive environment on places like YouTube, it has become increasingly more important to quickly grab people's attention and to get them engaged in your video content.

An easy way of doing that is to use short, well-crafted animated video clips at strategic places inside your videos. For example, using a short, 3-5 second animation of your logo (an intro) toward the start of your videos can help reset the attention of your viewers, thereby increasing the probability of them watching your video content for longer.

Additionally, using a little intro like this, can also easily and quickly instill your brand on a sub-conscious level without coming across tacky. Segueways serve a similar purpose to intros, except they are much shorter (only around half a second long) and are used throughout your whole video.

Use them sparingly in places where the attention of your viewer needs to get reset again. This will once again increase the probability of people watching your videos for much longer.

For example, segueways work great when moving from one topic or scene to the next inside your video.

Gideon Shalwick - Founder, www.splasheo.com

Video editing program options

38. Windows movie maker (for PC)

Windows Movie Maker is the most basic and rudimentary video editing program which today comes integrated on most new PCs. It allows you to perform basic editing like adding transitions or text onto your videos, but really is too simplistic for most small businesses. I would instead recommend obtaining Sony Vegas. To download Windows Movie Maker, go to:

http://windows.microsoft.com/en-US/windows/get-movie-maker-download

39. Sony Vegas (for PC)

If you want a more professional video editor you should look at Sony Vegas - widely used among many video producers with numerous features Windows Movie Makers does not have. There are different versions of this program, the cheapest one starting at $44.95 USD. You can find all of the available versions here:

http://www.sonycreativesoftware.com/vegassoftware

40. iMovie (for Mac)

iMovie comes integrated on all Mac computers and laptops, and lets you add professional looking titles, transitions, cut your clips, and share your videos on YouTube, Facebook, or Vimeo. However, on the Mac, I personally prefer to use ScreenFlow for most of my video editing. This alternative is much faster and more stable than iMovie. ScreenFlow also works perfectly for recording screen capture videos.

41. Final Cut Pro (for Mac)

Final Cut Pro is the gold standard in video editing software for the Mac. Made by Apple and used by editors and producers worldwide, Final Cut Pro is the tool used by true professionals to create stunning videos. Its feature list is extremely extensive (this is, after all, the tool used by Hollywood professionals), giving you the power to create high quality videos to promote your business. Whether it is creating trailers and advertisements for a new product, or producing special effects, you can do it all with Final Cut Pro. As you are starting out, there is a learning curve involved in order to learn how to use Final Cut Pro - be patient. Also consider just outsourcing your video editing if you are in a hurry (as most of us are).

SECTION 3 – YOUTUBE PROMOTION

YouTube optimization – Part 1

YouTube is the second most popular search engine. With more people preferring audio-visual content, its importance is growing every day. Particularly for small businesses, YouTube provides for a huge opportunity in setting your company apart from the competition as most still are not actively using its full potential or properly optimizing their videos.

YouTube offers a wide variety of options for marketers to optimize their videos for maximum views. The following lists the main strategies you should begin implementing.

42. Create professional looking channels

One of your first tasks should be signing up on YouTube. Personalize your channel to mirror the unique visual aspects of your company's website. You can upload a background and profile image, which will appear every time visitors leave comments on videos.

You are also provided a brief space to share some information about your company. Within this forum you can add links to your presence on other social media accounts like Facebook and Twitter, and also links directly to your website.

43. Correctly upload and optimize your videos

When uploading your videos, there are three main sections you need to optimize correctly.

First on the list is your video's title. The title should begin with the main keyword phrase you have set for ranking your video on search results. Remember the tips I had shared in the "planning" section of this book, and use those keywords you found using the tools indicated therein.

For most small companies, the most effective way to optimize YouTube video titles is by using the "sector + geo graphic location" within the text. So for instance, a restaurant in New York would have "restaurant in New York" as specific text within their title.

Additionally, you can add the phone number of your local business or some additional text to entice people to click and see the video. You can make changes to the keywords later from within your YouTube account.

Description

You should start this section with a link to your website or landing page, followed by a written description of what is included in the video. The keyword you have in the title can be repeated within the text for better optimization.

You can also add links to your social media accounts and encourage viewers to share the video in other social media. Visitors may even be enticed to insert your video in their own blog or website for further networking. This is a great way to increase the views of your YouTube video.

Tags

Include the most important keywords tags - significant phrases related to your video's topic. In addition, add your company's name into the tags. You can also use "standard tags" that will appear in each YouTube video. These can be setup inside your YouTube account; just go to "settings" and click on "defaults" under "channel settings".

44. Indicate your business's geographic location within the videos

The advanced settings on YouTube allow you to indicate where the video was recorded. The address can be geographically marked in your video. The image below shows exactly how this can be done.

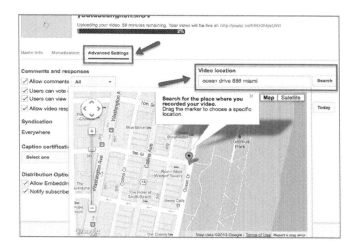

45. Add your videos to a playlist to maximize views

Each of your videos should be added to a playlist. This is simply a list of similar topic videos played in order. When watching a playlist, a viewer will automatically see one video after another since they start to play automatically. Therefore, it's very beneficial to create different playlists directing traffic towards your various videos. Under each video there is an "add to" button, which you can use to create a new playlist or add your video to a current playlist.

A company may choose to create a playlist for: testimonials, "how to" tutorials, employee presentations, company presentation videos, etc. Make sure each playlist has an interesting title, including some of the keywords relevant to your business.

YouTube optimization – Part 2

46. Prove your videos obtaining viewer comments and 'likes'

YouTube is constantly reworking their algorithms, which determine video ranking and traffic by increasing the importance of "social signals". Part of this equation relies on how often the video is shared on social media sites like Facebook and YouTube. The other part is based upon the amount of "likes" and comments that the video receives after it's uploaded onto YouTube. Under each video there is a button where visitors can subscribe to the channel and creator by clicking on "like".

The easiest way to improve this element is by always clicking 'like' on your video just after uploading it, and by leaving a comment under the video enticing people to give their opinion or ask questions in the comments section.

Under each video there is a counter to see how many times the video has been viewed and how many "likes" or "unlikes" the video has received. This has become an important social proof to some viewers in deciding whether they want to watch your video or not.

Therefore, you should be the first to like your own video. Encourage those on your company's mailing list or fans on other social networks like Facebook to also 'like' your video and leave comments and questions under it.

Another way of getting more "likes" and comment is simply by mentioning it at the end of your video. Business owners could say, "If you have any questions please call us at 111 222 333 (replace this with your real phone number) or leave your question on the comments section under this video."

"Likes and comments" are something you always want to increase. Be patient in the beginning since you probably won't have that many before building your community larger.

47. Encourage viewers to subscribe to your YouTube videos

Some of YouTube's top video producers obtain a huge number of views right after uploading their videos onto YouTube. This is mainly due to the large quantity of subscribers they have obtained.

One of my own channels has over 2,200 subscribers and, each time I upload a new video, these people will see it in their YouTube homepage when logged into their account. They will even see it on their mobile device.

The best way to get subscribers is by using annotations on the videos (I will talk more about this in the following section). People are able to click these and automatically subscribe to your videos. You should also place a link to subscribe in the description area under the video.

48. Add nice looking annotations to your video

As a small business, you normally want people to contact you directly after watching your marketing videos online. Perhaps the easiest way to encourage this is by getting them to call your phone number, so make sure to promote it in your uploads. I have already explained that you can add your phone number in the video's title and on YouTube's free annotations feature.

Avoid adding too many annotations though as this will decrease your video's overall quality. I recommend placing these in the corners of your video frames to avoid interfering with the viewer's ability to clearly see your video.

When logged into YouTube, an annotations button can be found at the top of each of your own videos.

As a small business owner, these are probably the most effective call to actions you can use in the annotations:

- – Encourage people to subscribe to your videos

- – Encourage people to call you

- Encourage people to follow your profile or business page on Google +

Eventually Google will also allow annotations to link to a website, but that feature is not yet active.

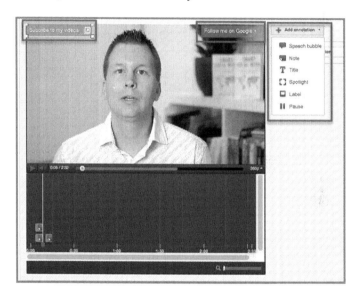

49. Improve your video's quality by editing or adding music

After uploading a video onto YouTube, you can change the info and settings of the video, enhance the quality, or add some audio track onto it.

Info and settings

This section allows you to change the title of the video and add text to your description. It also allows you to change some advanced settings like the location where the video was recorded, etc.

Enhancements

By using enhancements you can quickly improve the image quality of your video - change the contrast or saturation of the image, or even stabilize the frames if it recorded shaky. If you are using good quality camera like the Canon Rebel tI3, normally there will be no need to improve the quality. However, it's good to about know this option if you ever do need it. YouTube also has an editor which allows you to create video mash-ups mixing pieces of your videos and other features. This can be found at:

www.youtube.com/editor

Additional YouTube Marketing Strategies

50. Impress your customers by organizing live video conferences with "Google hangouts"

Even after seeing your videos on YouTube, many potential customers will still be wary about doing business with your company. With Google Hangouts, you will have an amazing opportunity to increase credibility and confidence with your audience by organizing live virtual events or online conferences, allowing people to see you live and even directly ask questions.

Some local companies have already started leveraging the many benefits Google Hangouts provides, including:

- Showcasing your new products and answering live any questions your customers might have

- Having special monthly Q & A sessions with your audience

- Being able to share the recorded video of your online conference on YouTube right after it's done

In order to start using Google Hangouts you will need to create an account on Google Plus and connect it with your YouTube channel. This will enable people to view your video conferences live.

Once you have a Google + account, you can test it out by going to *https://plus.google.com/hangouts* and clicking on the link "start a hangout"

Up to 10 people can simultaneously speak and show their faces on the Hangout, and the organizer can opt to share his screen or any document.

Google Hangouts is being used by Google to transmit large events live. And now, companies can start using this amazing feature totally for free.

You can learn more about Google Hangouts here:

http://www.google.com/+/learnmore/hangouts/

51. Encourage people to share the video

Some small businesses erroneously consider YouTube to be just another bulletin board where they can upload videos for immediate viewing. This is wrong for a few reasons.

In video marketing and social media, one of your most valuable assets will be strategic relationships and partnerships with influential people in your market place.

Let's say you are an immigration lawyer wanting to improve your marketing and presence on YouTube. I would suggest creating a series of high quality "how to" tutorials on immigration law and then offering them to some websites or blogs receiving the most traffic on this topic. Most website owners are always looking for additional valuable content and would be happy to have this mutually beneficial relationship. You can simply do a search on Google, YouTube, or other social media sites, and find the biggest influencers. Talk with them and create a relationship; offer your generic video tutorials for their blogs and websites. You can also interview them or find other creative ways to work collaboratively.

Additionally, you can mention in your video's description area that anyone is free to share it on their social media sites, or embed the video in their own blog or website.

As a rule of thumb, the better the videos you make, the more people that are likely to share them.

52. Add video transcriptions to enhance your video's ranking

An extra strategy that many top YouTube contributors apply is transcribing the video's audio into a written text format (there are several services online which can do this for a minimal price). This feature can also be used to create subtitles for your videos.

Transcriptions can easily be added by clicking on "captions" in the same bar above each of your videos (when you are logged into YouTube) where you find "info and settings", "enhancements", "audio" and "annotations" - as all discussed in the previous section.

After clicking on "captions" on the next page, you have the option to "upload caption file or transcript". By clicking on that you can then upload your file to a video

YouTube recommends uploading the transcription in a plain text file and avoiding any special characters.

53. Increase your views with "Google Adwords"

YouTube is always adding new options for incorporating paid advertising into your videos. You may also pay to 'promote' your videos to a specific audience. The official name for this service is "Google Adwords for video". You will first need to create a Google Adwords account and then connect it to your YouTube account. You can learn more about this feature and how to create your account by visiting:

www.google.com/ads/video

In the following image you can see two videos, which populated first when searching the keyword "New York Dentist"

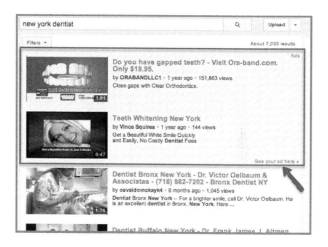

The best way to take advantage of Google Ads for video is by testing it out on a small budget, using only your most valuable keywords. This will normally constitute your activity and geographical location.

You can learn more about YouTube video advertising at:

www.youtube.com/yt/advertise/promote.html

YouTube partner techniques

YouTube has a partner program which allows its members to enjoy some additional features that normal users don't have. Not many companies are part of the partner program yet, however, you might consider joining if your company is continuously adding new content. Just make sure to read up on and abide by the community guidelines (more information can be found here:

https://www.youtube.com/t/community_guidelines),

including things like not using copyrighted material on your videos, etc.

To learn more on how to become a partner, visit:

http://www.youtube.com/account_monetization

The following are some advantages to holding a partner account.

54. Set attractive looking thumbnails onto your videos

Automatically, after uploading your video, YouTube allows you to choose one thumbnail image among 3 different options (this can be found under "info and settings). However, partners are able to upload their own thumbnail images, allowing for a more attractive visual than the default images provided to standard users.

Creating a clear and attractive thumbnail image will increase your video views. Those who come across that image of your video on Google or YouTube search results are far more likely to click on it if it looks attractive and interesting.

Here is an example of a video by Redbull found on Google's search engine. Notice where they have added the word "exclusive" to the video image.

As a partner, you can upload an image to the "info and settings" area by clicking on "custom thumbnail".

55. Schedule your videos for more exposure

As your audience and community grow it will become more important to be consistent in uploading videos onto YouTube. Schedule your uploads to be optimized at a time when most of your target audience is likely to be online.

As with Facebook and Twitter, I would recommend adding your videos on weekends during the morning hours, ideally between 10.00 am and 1:00 am. This will allow you to later share the videos on Twitter and Facebook, and encourage others to share them as well and leave comments.

Regarding video production, the most effective use of your company's time and resources will be spent by recording several videos at once. Once you are a YouTube partner, simply schedule your videos so that they will be publicly available at certain times during the morning regular office hours.

In order to schedule your videos, simply click on "upload" at the top of the YouTube page and select "scheduled", as shown in the following image. Then just simply follow the steps as indicated.

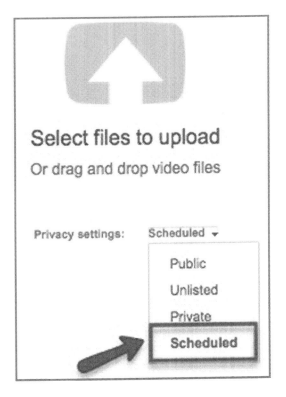

56. Put clickable links in your YouTube videos using YouTube annotations

This is a very powerful feature that allows you put links in your YouTube videos. It can be applied when you have a partner channel, basically allowing you to insert

annotations into your videos with links to your website
that needs to be associated with your YouTube channel.

57. Insert your logo and featured video in all of your videos

This next feature is actually available to all YouTube
accounts. It's called "in video programming" and basically
allows you to insert your own logo into each of your
YouTube videos. It also lets you create permits to use a
featured video - shown and promoted in all of your
YouTube videos with a small thumbnail in the corner, as
indicated in the image below.

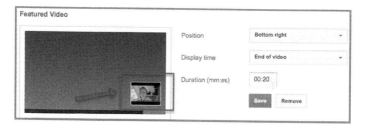

This option can be found where you setup featured videos,
simply by clicking on "settings" and then "in video
programming" under "channel settings".

To enhance a company's video branding, some choose to
add their logo onto all videos using the featured channel
option.

This is simply an image or logo of your company with a
link to your company's channel.

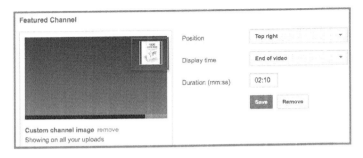

Both of these features are highly recommended to all those who want to leverage YouTube marketing to its highest potential.

I should also add that in the same area, just under the "in video programming" option, you have an "add associated link". This enables you to add a link that will be connected to your YouTube account. For most companies, this link directs to an official website. At some point going forward, YouTube will allow you to link directly to your website from your YouTube annotations, making it possible to give very powerful calls to action on your videos.

Improve your result with YouTube video analytics

One of the biggest challenges that small business owners face with video marketing is correctly understanding and analyzing results. On a monthly basis, someone should analyze the effectiveness of your YouTube videos and generate the various reports available in the "analytics" section.

I have provided below some of the most important metrics and you will need to learn how this data is analyzed to determine improvements in video marketing activities.

58. Discover the overall analytics on YouTube

YouTube analytics displays several interesting indicators on the performance of your company's videos. Two of the main analytics you will come across are "performance" and "engagement".

Performance will show how many views you received last month (or whichever timeframe you choose) and how many estimated minutes have been watched. If you are part of the YouTube monetization program, you can also see your total estimated earnings.

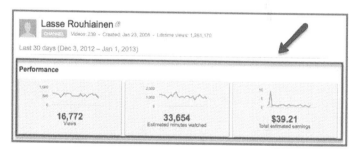

The monthly views data is very important and something you want to pay attention to. Try to find action items that can help you to increase your views.

Another important visual illustration of your overall analytics is "engagement". This series will indicate all the following data: new likes, new dislikes, number of comments, number of shares, how many people have favorite your videos, and also how many new subscribers you have gained.

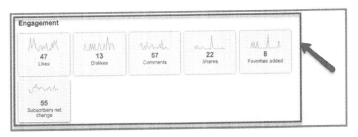

As I mentioned in the previous section, you should encourage people to 'like' and comment on your videos, share them on Facebook, and also click to subscribe.

I also advise all of my consulting clients to analyze their videos which have received the highest amount of "dislikes". This will normally be a clear indication of where you need improvement - for instance, that the video was not properly titled to reflect the content. You can take this information and learn from your mistakes to improve future videos, in both their format and structure.

59. Rank your videos better by analyzing the "average view duration" metrics

Considering the video ranking algorithm on YouTube, "average view duration" might be the most important indicator to analyze.

Currently, YouTube ranks the best videos according to those watched until the end (in some cases this is even more important than using the right keywords in the title of your videos).

Here is an example of how YouTube presents the "average view duration" from one of my own YouTube channels. This indicates that the average viewer will watch 2 minutes of my videos and then leave.

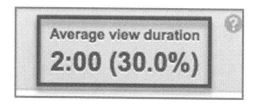

Many of my videos are 4 to 6 minutes long, some even longer. By seeing this data I conclude that my viewers prefer shorter content. I can then improve my videos by tailoring them to this trait, recording videos, which are only 2 minutes, or less.

This improvement will also help to increase their rank within YouTube. As mentioned before, one of the most important ranking factors on YouTube currently is whether people will watch your video through to the end.

60. Analyze your Traffic sources and make improvements

The next metric to analyze is "traffic sources". This source shows exactly where your videos obtain most of their viewer traffic. This is extremely beneficial information not to be underestimated. The image below presents the traffic sources for one of my own channels over the last few months.

Traffic source	Views ↓	Estimated minutes watched
External website	27,838 (31.9%)	13,147 (32.7%)
YouTube search	20,991 (24.1%)	9,616 (23.9%)
Google search	13,963 (16.0%)	4,058 (10.1%)
Mobile apps and direct traffic (unknown sources)	12,959 (14.9%)	6,391 (15.9%)
YouTube suggested video	7,991 (9.2%)	5,846 (14.5%)
Embedded player (unknown sources)	2,144 (2.5%)	927 (2.3%)

The data goes so far as to even show a percentage. We can see that "external websites", "YouTube search", and "Google search" accounted for most of my viewer traffic.

You can click on each of these areas below to obtain more details. For example, when clicking on "Google Search" you will see exactly which keywords contributed to your ranking on Google and generated visits to your videos.

You can make changes to the titles and descriptions of your videos to optimize them even better on the front page of Google's search engine. This will also let people more easily and readily find your content.

61. Analyze the demographic and geographic data of your audience

In the first section of this book, I highlighted the importance of determining your ideal client in order to generate interesting and valuable content tailored for them.

Demographic and geographic data reveals interesting insights and helps your company to see if you are reaching your ideal customer.

This section in analytics show the percentage of your viewers who are male or female, their age, and the geographical location from where they watched the videos.

YouTube also allows you to see different variations and to analyze your statistics in different time ranges, or even by viewers in different countries.

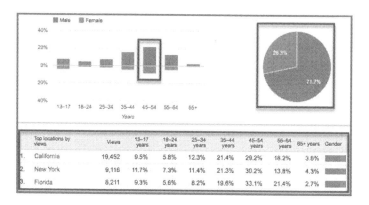

The above image is an example representation of my viewers in the United States. You can clearly see that the average viewer is a male, between the ages of 45 – 54, and either lives in California, New York, or Florida.

This information is extremely useful and I can leverage it by saying something in my future videos important to people who live in those areas. Alternatively, I can create specific tutorials directed to them.

In addition, your company can use this information to target these demographics when conducting Facebook advertising or any other type of online advertising.

SECTION 4 – ADDITIONAL VIDEO STRATEGIES

Get your videos shared on Facebook

Facebook is the largest social media site with over one billion users. Your company should take advantage of this by creating a powerful presence on Facebook using a professionally created business page. You can discover all of the main strategies I recommend in my book, "Smart Social Media - Your Guide To Becoming A Highly Paid Social Media Manager".

By following the four techniques outlined below, you can vastly improve your videos' success on Facebook and gain a competitive edge against your competition.

62. Share your videos the right way on Facebook

The most common activity on Facebook and which users are most familiar with is photo sharing.

As a marketer, you should recognize trend and be sure to avoid the more common mistakes when uploading videos to Facebook. That is, don't upload lengthy videos which take more time to understand than your viewers have the attention span for. One good tip is to indicate the video's purpose right away in the intro of the video so that the audience knows exactly what to expect.

As Facebook users are used to quickly seeing photos and leaving comments, they need a compelling reason to stop and watch your videos. Even more so, they need a reason to share it with others.

Therefore, only upload your best videos onto Facebook - those which are short and to the point, teach something interesting, or are funny and original.

Facebook allows you to share your YouTube videos directly as a link or you can upload the original video file source. Most of the time it's best to just upload your video file because this allows you to more easily incorporate ads if you want to promote that video.

When posting a video, always ask some question that Facebook users can easily answer in the comments. Additionally, try to encourage people to share the video with their Facebook friends.

63. Showcase your YouTube videos with a YouTube tab on your Facebook page

Some visitors to your Facebook page will want to know more information about your company. Therefore, it's recommended that you incorporate an application which professionally showcases your latest YouTube videos.

Many companies use the Facebook application by Involver to show all of their latest videos. You can find this application here:

http://www.involver.com/applications/

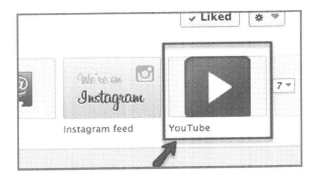

64. Use photos to promote your videos

Some companies successfully use photos on Facebook to promote videos posted on their website. Steps for implementing this include:

1. Create great looking images with a title of your video and something that catches attention.

2. Post those images on your Facebook page with text about the video, and encourage people to share and comment on the post.

Below is an example on how Marie Forleo does this on her great Facebook page:

www.facebook.com/marieforleo

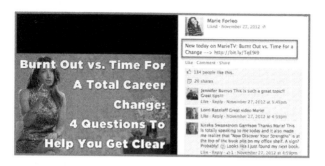

As you can see, many of her followers like her content, leave comments, and share it with others.

65. Take advantage of the "promoted post" advertising feature on Facebook

Facebook pages with more than 400 likes are able to promote any posts that they have made - whether it is text, photo, or video. You can designate a budget for extra promotion of posts which highlighting your videos by using "promoted post".

Typically, fans of your Facebook page will not see the videos or posts you publish. By using this feature you can be sure to promote your content and increase its visibility among your viewers.

One of the most significant benefits of using "promoted post" is that the content will appear in the normal newsfeed on Facebook - not on the side column where other advertising is placed. Therefore, to most Facebook users, this does not appear as advertising but as normal Facebook activity.

Share your video on the main social media sites

66. Discover the power of sharing your video on Google +

Google´s own social network, called Google + (or Google Plus), is playing an increasingly important role in social media. Google is using Google + as a central hub to all of their other Google services. For example, in order to change your photo on YouTube, you need to do from within your Google + account. Google + is also gaining more importance regarding search engine optimization. For example, content that is shared most within Google +

will normally get a better ranking on Google's search engine.

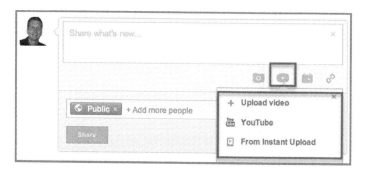

For that reason, it's important that you try to use Google + every time and share your YouTube videos on your Google Plus profile and business page (which your company should have).

As with Facebook, when you share your video, try to get users to leave a comment or to share content within Google +.

67. Leverage the growing popularity of Pinterest

Throughout 2012, Pinterest became the fastest growing social media site, especially popular among female online users. Companies with visually attractive products or services like restaurants, tourism companies, pastry shops, etc, should consider creating a presence on Pinterest.

Traditionally, Pinterest was created to share and comment, and to create photo boards (called pin boards). Now, companies are also allowed to post YouTube videos on their Pinterest accounts.

To correctly share your videos on Pinterest, always use the main video url and not the embed HTML code. Every video's main url can be found under the "share" button, just below the video - as shown in this example below.

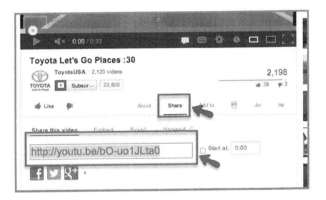

If your company has an account on Pinterest, you can click "add" on the top of any Pinterest page and then select "add a pin" to simply insert YouTube url link for the video you want to share. Then just write a description and click on "pin it".

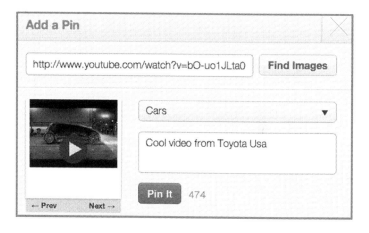

Pinterest is gaining more and more relevance among the important social media sites and you should consider creating a presence if you have visually-oriented products or a services.

68. Get your videos shared on Twitter

Twitter is a great service for journalists, sports people, and social media consultant. However, not many small businesses know how to leverage the power of Twitter the right way.

If you have a Twitter account I highly recommend that you share all your videos on there. However, don't fall trap to the same mistakes most small companies make who treat Twitter like just another bulletin board. Instead, be conversational - pose questions, start discussions, respond to comments. Also, share your videos with posed question to start an interesting conversation among your followers.

To facilitate sharing your videos on Twitter, you can connect your company's Twitter account with your YouTube channel. When uploading a video, it will automatically then be shared on Twitter. Just write a brief text where it says, "post to your subscribers" and select the Twitter icon as demonstrated in the image above.

Always try to keep the message under 120 characters so that people can easily re-tweet them on Twitter (sending the same message to their own followers).

69. Share your videos on LinkedIn

LinkedIn is the largest social network among business professionals. In particular, service companies and B2B companies numerous networking opportunities inside LinkedIn.

You can share videos in your status updates on LinkedIn or links to YouTube videos inside some special groups. However, always make sure that you only share the most valuable content, that which is original or interesting to the particular users, to optimize their reception. For example, special tutorial videos might be especially well received among LinkedIn's users.

LinkedIn offers small businesses the ability to create company pages to amplify their presence and showcase information about their activity. However, as of now, there is currently no option for sharing videos on these company pages.

Smart business professionals who want to improve their branding share YouTube videos in their LinkedIn profile by using an application from SlideShare.

Increase your sales using video email strategies

Probably the least used video marketing strategy is video email with your clients and business partners. With the use of video, you can take your company's email communications to the next level by "humanizing" your communications. This method allows people to see and hear you rather than just reading a text written by you.

I have personally used video email for the last 4 years when communicating with important clients and sharing information with my team. Every time I want to re-establish some old relationship with someone, I will send them a video email instead of just normal text.

In addition to following up or sending proposals to clients, companies can use video emails for customer support or simply sending "thank you videos" to their best customers.

70. Set yourself apart with a great webcam

Before creating video emails, make sure your company has a professional webcam which records in full HD. Some new PCs or Macs might have this integrated already. If not, you might consider either the Logitech HD Pro Webcam C920 or Microsoft LifeCam Studio 1080p HD Webcam. Both of these record in 1080p HD and have superior image quality.

You need to safeguard your brand image and set your company apart by using a high quality web cam. Avoid putting out low quality images like some of your competitors might be using.

71. Use a clean and professional background with the proper lighting

When filming a video email, make sure the person speaking is nicely dressed and presents in front of a clear and professional background. I recommend companies use backgrounds, which are spacious, avoiding dull, open walls. This applies to video emails for customer support, sending proposals to potential clients, and any other uses you might find for them.

Additionally, make sure you use good lighting. I recommend the same lighting kit I had mentioned in an earlier section when discussing the various lighting options.

72. Create video emails on the go using your smartphone

As the use of mobile phones and tablets grows among business people, you need to educate your personnel on how to shoot videos using their smartphones or tablets. This is a powerful way to keep in contact with important customers or partners, even while travelling.

I personally recommend using Gudymail, found at _www.gudymail.com_. Full disclosure, I'm a business adviser to Gudymail so my opinion is biased. Regardless of my connections, I have found that they have the best iPhone and iPad apps for video email. There are numerous professional features that business professionals can take advantage of for everyday uses.

When using devices such as the iPhone for video email, try to use a tripod (more about this in the next section of this book). Also, incorporate interesting looking backgrounds if at all possible. The best way to learn this is by using video email within the company, sending videos to employees and other personnel. Analyze how they look in this safe environment, sharing your ideas on how to improve them.

73. Analyze your statistics and be consistent

When using video email, make sure you are consistent and always follow up on the messages you have created. The real effectiveness of a video email is ability to always see the statistics. These illustrate whether your video has been viewed and, if so, how many times.

The ability to access statistics is particularly powerful for consultants sending video proposals; when constantly presenting yourself and offering your services to start commercial relationships, it's essential to know how you are being received. One place where consultants are doing this effectively is on LinkedIn. When sending this kind of video email to cold contacts who don't know you, you will immediately see from the statistics how many people have viewed your video and, therefore, can follow up with the ones who have.

When viewing the statistics in the gudymail.com dashboard, I sometimes see some of my videos being viewed 7 or 10 times by the same people - those impressed by being able to see and hear me rather than just read my emails.

Discover different video hosting options

74. Vimeo Pro

Some companies create protected members areas for their clients inside their website to share special videos - those which, for one reason or another, are not offered publicly. This is a professional way of providing more value to your clients. Offering this may provide an incentive for clients to buy a certain service.

For instance, consulting firms could have their "clients only area" for sharing strategies not otherwise provided publicly on YouTube. Or, they could show a finalized project to some specific clients. Simply upload your videos to Vimeo and then insert the embedded code into your website's protected client area.

One of the most widely used services to host your company videos is called Vimeo Pro. This program is directed towards businesses wanting to share commercial videos and it provides several useful features for this audience - such as professional protection of your videos, customization of your embedded video player, and being able to upload 50 gb of video content (with the option to buy more, if needed).

All of the videos loaded on Vimeo can be viewed on an iPhone or iPad, providing a huge plus against other similar services. Currently, the cost of Vimeo Pro is 159 euros per year. You can find more information at:

www.vimeo.com/pro

75. Analyze your landing page videos with Wistia

Wistia is one of the most popular video hosting services among marketers and businesses who use landing page videos and need advanced statistics to analyze the effectiveness of their videos.

Wistia has maybe the most advanced video statistics and easily provides the ability to see at what time cutoff people stop watching your videos (fundamental data for you to analyze).

You can start with Wistia for free and host up to 3 videos. You can learn more about the pricing and features at:

http://wistia.com

76. Amazon S3

Amazon s3 (Simple Storage Service) is a cloud-based service which allows companies to upload unlimited videos to their service. You will only be charged for the amount of bandwidth used, meaning the amount of time people watch your videos.

I used this service myself for many years while hosting my online courses. However, services like Vimeo Pro have many advantages over this program making it a more likely alternative than first choice. For example, the being able to upload any video file or view them on iPhone and iPad makes Vimeo a better choice.

You can learn more about Amazon s3 video hosting at:

http://aws.amazon.com/s3/

77. Dropbox

When you need to share video files with your clients or partners, Dropbox offers the best option. This service allows you to store and share files of any type, and to easily access them with your computer or mobile device.

Most of the time you cannot send video files directly as an email attachment due to their large file size. DropBox provides a workaround to this and is easy to use across multiple devices, like the iPhone or iPad. You can start with a free account and learn more about DropBox at:

http://www.dropbox.com

Sell more products with Webinar strategies

Webinars are online seminars where companies showcase a new product or teach something interesting. Participants can see the screen, hear the presenter's voice, post questions, and interact.

Webinars serve as one of the most powerful platforms for selling products and are becoming especially popular among software companies or tech start-ups. These fields, and those like them, particularly benefit from connecting and interacting with their audience on a consistent basis. Likewise, lawyers, accountants, health professionals, and virtually any business professional can benefit from using webinars for 'question and answer' sessions with their customers. One of the best benefits of webinars is that they are very cost effective, and eliminate the necessity of organizing expensive offline meetings and presentations with your potential customers.

The following are some of the most powerful webinar platforms that you can evaluate, choosing the most appropriate for your particular business needs.

78. Google Hangout

Like I had mentioned before, Google Hangout is a very powerful and free online conference service from Google. Simply create a Google + account and connect it with your YouTube channel.

The most powerful feature of this service is "Google Hangouts Live", allowing you to stream your conferences live on YouTube and record them as a YouTube video.

When using Google Hangouts, I recommend creating a clean environment in the background of your office; people will see you via your webcam and you want to give a good impression of your working space. Also, be sure to prepare some interesting PowerPoint slides that you can present to the participants. You might also consider using webinarjam.com, which allows you to use Google Hangouts with a lot of extra features and benefits.

79. Gotomeeting

Gotomeeting and its sister service, GotoWebinar, are both provided by the same company, "Citrix". These are two of the most robust and well-respected platforms for delivering your webinars. Through these services, viewers only see your computer screen. They then participate by using a microphone or sending questions in a chat window.

The programs can both record a copy of your webinar to be shown to the people who registered but were unable to participate.

When planning your webinars, I would suggest starting with quick 30 to 40 minute webinars. Shorter sessions make it easier for the audience to participate the whole time.

Gotomeeting and gotowebinar participants can join via iPhone and iPad applications. For professional sessions of almost any company, I would list Gotomeeting and GotoWebinar as the most recommended. More information can be found at:

www.gotomeeting.com

80. Meetingburner

Meetingburner is a similar service to GotoMeeting and Gotowebinar, however, it is not quite as robust. This is a better option for companies just getting started, charging a lower price per each attendee than comparable programs. MeetingBurner offers mobile attendee support and is compatible with either a MAC or PC. The free

conference room with Meetingburner can hold up to 10 attendees. More information about this webinar service can be found at:

www.meetingburner.com

81. Anymeeting

Anymeeting is a similar service to Meetingburner, holding up to 200 attendees for free in each conference room. Note, however, that these rooms are advertisement supported. Anymeeting has a video group chat feature similar to Google Hangouts, and is very widely used among many business professionals. You can learn more about Anymeeting at:

www.anymeeting.com

SECTION 5: IPHONE VIDEO MARKETING STRATEGIES

Get the right iPhone accessories for video marketing

By far, the one aspect of video marketing I find most exciting when looking to the future is mobile video marketing - recording, editing, and sharing videos easily and quickly with gadgets like the iPhone and iPad.

Mobile video marketing provides a huge opportunity for small businesses because so many business owners now carry Smartphones, like the iPhone 5, which record superior full HD videos. With tools like these you can now film and share like a pro while only knowing the most basic operations.

This section is heavily focused on the iPhone and iPad for the simple reason that the most powerful accessories and applications are normally made first for these devices, only later opening up to other smartphones and tablet computers.

Whether you are just starting to use your smartphone for your business or have been a longtime user, I'm sure that you will find valuable content and ideas in this section.

Try to apply them as soon as possible - before your competitors do.

If you are using the iPhone 4s or iPhone 5, you have the capability to record very professional quality videos everywhere you go. With the right video accessories you can take your iPhone video marketing to the next level.

82. Purchase a professional microphone for your iPhone

The latest versions of the iPhone have built-in microphones which record acceptable video and audio quality. However, to record more professional videos for your business, you will need an external microphone accessory.

The Mikey Digital Recording Microphone for the Apple iPhone by Blue is one of the best options and allows you to record very high quality audio with your iPhone. This device plugs directly into the iPhone making it simple to use as well.

The iRig Handheld Mic for the iPhone by IK multimedia is the best option if your focus is on video interviews with clients, collaborating with partners, or just everyday videos. Depending on your goals, this might be the right iPhone microphone for you.

You can also use any other microphone mentioned in the previous sections of this book. For instance, the Sony ECM-AW3 Wireless Microphone works well, but you will have to purchase an additional adapter like the iPhone 1/8 inch microphone adapter from kvconnection.com. This adapter is a very handy tool regardless because it allows you to use almost any microphone with your iPhone. All of the microphones mentioned in this section can be found on Amazon.com.

83. Use an image stabilizer for smooth filming

One of the challenges in filming with an iPhone is that it is not made specifically for recording professional videos. Therefore, it can be a bit clumsy to hold and, often times, will visibly show shaking.

There are two solutions for this problem. First, you can purchase a LiveAction Camera Grip by Belkin. This is an adjustable grip that enables you to firmly hold the camera, making it feel and film more like a professional device. It has an integrated tripod mount, making it compatible with any tripod, and doesn't require purchasing a special tripod for the iPhone.

Another option is to purchase the Slingshot Smartphone

Video Stabilizer by woxom. This is a handheld gadget helping you to better hold the iPhone while filming videos, as shown in the image below.

Slingshot also allows you to use the iPhone's front-facing camera and shoot stable videos of yourself talking. The cradle can be unscrewed for use with any tripod.

84. Use a tripod when shooting videos with your iPhone

As with normal video cameras, you should consider using a tripod when recording videos. As I mentioned before, gadgets like the Slingshot and LiveAction Camera Grip can be used with any tripod. The most popular iPhone specific tripod is the Glif Tripod Mount by Studio Neat.

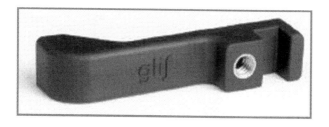

85. Take your iPhone recording to the next level with the Swivl Personal Cameraman

This is maybe the most innovative iPhone or iPad video accessory, essentially mandatory for anyone wanting the best possible filming from their device. The Swivl Personal Cameraman by Satarii, Inc. is a particularly handy gadget when recording lectures or presentations.

Swivl automatically follows you both horizontally and vertically so that you can give lectures without the need of a cameraman. It also comes with a wireless microphone.

As it's a bit difficult to explain with mere text, here is a link to a video promotion by Engadget illustrating just how Swivl works: http://youtu.be/Nys4yPlEn_U

Tips for recording your company videos on the iPhone

86. Treat it like a video camera

Recording videos with your iPhone can help you save a considerable amount of time and resources. However, it's crucial that you have the proper lighting, the right microphone, an interesting background, a tripod (I provide some options in the next section), and all of the other things you would normally use with a standard video camera. Today, there is a wide array of available accessories available to help you easily make superior quality videos on the iPhone. I provide many of the best options, along with critiques, in the next section.

87. Hold the camera horizontally

Avoid the common mistake most businesses commit when recording videos on the iPhone for the first time - don't hold it vertically. The problem you later face doing this is that, on YouTube, a video recorded vertically will have big black areas on the left and right margins. YouTube always shows videos horizontally, creating gaps in alignment transitioning.

Therefore, make sure you always hold your camera horizontally when recording. This becomes even easier once you've acquired some of the tools I illustrate in the next section for making your videos more stable.

88. Ensure your iPhone has enough free memory

This is perhaps the biggest challenge I often face because

I tend to shoot a lot of pictures and short video clips. Occasionally my iPhone's memory capacity is completely full.

For a Mac, "image capture" can quickly transfer all of your videos onto the computer's hard drive (typically into your applications folder).Just connect your phone to your

Mac with a standard cable and it will let you copy the videos you want onto your computer.

To transfer videos and photos wirelessly, the best option is to use the Photo Sync app. This program costs $1.99 USD on the app store and allows you to quickly share your videos and photos with either your PC or Mac. In order to receive the photos you will also have to download the Photo Sync program onto your computer, which can be found here:

http://www.photosync-app.com/

In addition to saving the videos on your computer, remember to save one copy of them on an external hard drive as well as a backup - just in case something happens to the original files.

89. Use the iPhone 5's built-in focus capability

The iPhone 5 has lets you tap the screen where the person is talking on the video and automatically adjust the lighting. This allows you to make sure that the video is always in focus. Things like these are tiny details but which make a huge difference in the overall quality when watching your videos online.

Use the most powerful video marketing iPhone applications – Part I

90. View and capture videos with YouTube video applications

Currently, YouTube has two very powerful applications designed for the iPhone. The main app is simply called the "YouTube application", which allows you to browse and search your favorite videos or see new video postings on subscribed YouTube channels. This app is fast and easy to use, and I highly recommend you install it for video marketing. Get the app here:

https://itunes.apple.com/en/app/youtube/id544007664?mt=8

Interested in quickly recording videos and immediately sharing them on YouTube? "YouTube Capture" is an innovative app from Google which allows you to record a video and share it immediately on YouTube, as well as on Google +, Twitter, and Facebook.

One feature I find useful is that I can access previously recorded videos on my iPhone and upload them to YouTube. This is particularly helpful when travelling or visiting some events where you don't have an internet connection.

"YouTube Capture" is probably the most important video marketing app for small businesses and definitely the one you want learn for quick video recording and sharing by your company.

You can find the app here:

https://itunes.apple.com/us/app/youtube-capture/id576941441

91. Edit your videos with iMovie

iMovie enables fast video editing with the iPhone and permits you to add titles, transitions, and soundtracks to your videos. You can also instantaneously share your videos on YouTube.

iMovie is by far the most well known iPhone video editing program and a must-have for most companies. You should take the time to familiarize yourself with it for use when you need to add titles or transitions to your videos.

iMovie is a paid app and currently costs $4.99 USD. You can get it here:

https://itunes.apple.com/en/app/imovie/id377298193?mt=8

92. Create professional slideshow videos with the Animoto app

Animoto is a leading company for creating professional slideshow videos, as mentioned in the previous section of this book. Their iPhone app allows you to create stunning videos with music and text, especially useful for tourism companies and restaurants. It is also quite helpful for covering any events where you shoot photos to later be compiled as a nice looking slideshow video. The new version of the Animoto iPhone app also enables you to quickly share on Facebook. The Animoto application is available for both Android and iPhone operating systems

93. Create nice looking video presentations with Videolicious

Videolicious is nice little app that can mix your photos and video clips into professional looking videos with voiceover. This program can be used for showcasing your offices, restaurant, or shop interiors, or any other video presentations. It is also handy for sales pitching and video interviews. With Videolicious, you can add licensed music and share your videos on social networks, like Twitter and Facebook.

Together with YouTube capture, Videolicious is the most suitable app for most small businesses wanting to create super fast professional videos showcasing their company. Videolicious is only available for iPhone operating system.

Use the most powerful video marketing iPhone applications - Part II

94. Filmic Pro

One of the most advanced iPhone apps for video recording, Filmic Pro enables you to use some cool presets. For example, you can record your videos in 24p, 25p or 30p, or decide whether you want to record in slow or fast motion. You can also control the volume level, focus, exposure, white balance, and frame rates. The slow and fast motion options are especially useful and help you to create cool looking videos of your products and services.

Additionally, you can zoom while recording your video, and set up a whole host of other professional settings. The app even allows you to share the videos automatically on YouTube, Facebook, Vimeo, and DropBox.

95. Almost DLSR

Similar to Filmic Pro, the Almost DSLR app allows you to use very powerful settings on your iPhone for video filming - such as focus, exposure, white balance, and many others as illustrated in the image below. However, I personally prefer Filmic Pro over Almost DSLR.

Almost DLSR is only available for iPhone operating system.

96. Slow Pro app

For creative videos, SloPro is an interesting, free option. This app allows you to record videos in fast motion, slow motion, or even super slow motion- very cool options for sport and recreation focused companies.

Slow Pro app is only available for Iphone, but there is a similar kind of application called Slo Motion Pro for Android operating system.

97. iMovie

As for iPhone apps, iMovie is the most well-know and commonly used video editing application for the iPad. It's definitely to your advantage that you obtain a copy of this app if using your iPad for filming videos. Personally, I enjoy using iMovie more on my iPhone and iPad than on my Mac computer. With the latest version of iMovie, you can perform all of the most important video editing effects and actions for a professional looking end-product. It should definitely be a primary option when considering video editing applications for the iPhone.

98. Pinnacle Studio

Pinnacle Studio is perhaps one of the most competitive applications to iMovie when it comes to video editing. With all of the possible features and effects, the only downside to Pinnacle Studio is the price. The app is currently selling for $12.99 as compared to $4.99 for iMovie. Pinnacle studio is only available for iPhone

99. Magisto

One of the most versatile video editing applications, Magisto is easy to use and allows you to quickly create professional looking footage from videos stored on your iPad. As with other video editing apps, you can easily add transitions, filters, and transitions, and comes with several nice looking themes to choose from.

Magisto is available for both Android and iPhone operating systems.

100. Splice

Splice has many similar features to Magisto with the added ability to insert voice-overs and perform audio editing. It's a decent video editing tool, however, iMovie, Pinnacle Studio, and Magisto tend to be more popular among people editing videos with their iPhones.

Splice is available for both Android and iPhone operating systems.

101. Take action!

When it comes to video marketing, perhaps the two most important words are "take action". Most of us are clueless on how to start or have a fear of failure. Like the slogan from Nike says, "Just Do It". If you fell stuck, take baby steps every day and think how you can improve the planning, recording, and promotion of your business.

About the author

Lasse Rouhiainen is an international video marketing and social media marketing expert and trainer, and frequent speaker at business schools and universities on the topics of YouTube, Facebook, and social media marketing.

Lasse is an author of an Amazon best selling book, "Smart Social Media - Your Guide To Becoming A Highly Paid Social Media Manager," and enjoys inspiring and educating entrepreneurs and small businesses on the topics of social media and video marketing.

Contact Lasse for a free consultation on how to create a video marketing strategy for your company.

www.lasserouhiainen.com

Video presentation about Lasse here:

www.youtube.com/watch?v=VuhXhRpbFvU

Review this book on Amazon

If you liked this book or found it useful in any way, please take a brief moment to review it on Amazon. Your feedback will help me to make it even better for future readers.

Thanks and good luck,

Lasse Rouhiainen

Made in the USA
Lexington, KY
06 February 2014